£ 2·50

CONTENTS

WRITTEN BY EVE SUMNER
DESIGN AND ILLUSTRATIONS
EDGAR HODGES

Published in Great Britain by
Stafford Pemberton Publishing, The Ruskin Chambers,
Drury Lane, Knutsford, Cheshire, WA16 6HA
Printed in Italy.
ISBN 0 86030 320 9.

STAFFORD PEMBERTON PUBLISHING

METAL MICKEY
Annual
1982

MEET METAL MICKEY

Metal Mickey has been around for quite some time but he refuses to give his age! He says it's somewhere between Donny Osmond's and Jimmy Young's! He has been treading the boards for several years. Before he became a 'superstar' he was a dustbin. It is rumoured he lived behind 'Harrods' along with several other dustbins.

When Humphrey Barday, London Weekend Television's Head of Comedy met Metal Mickey he said "I knew Mickey had star potential when I first met him. He has a fantastic personality and he is going to be a big hit with viewers of all ages!"

I think everyone would agree, Mickey's situation comedy series has been a huge success.

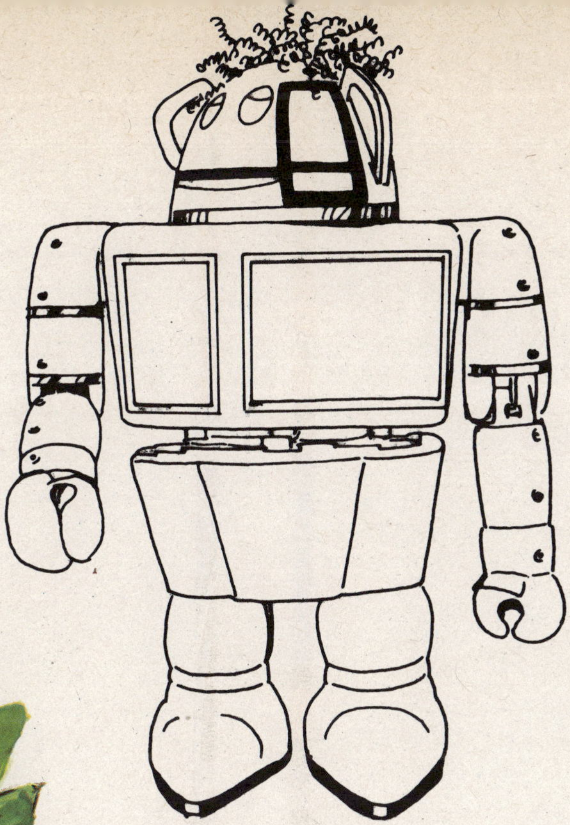

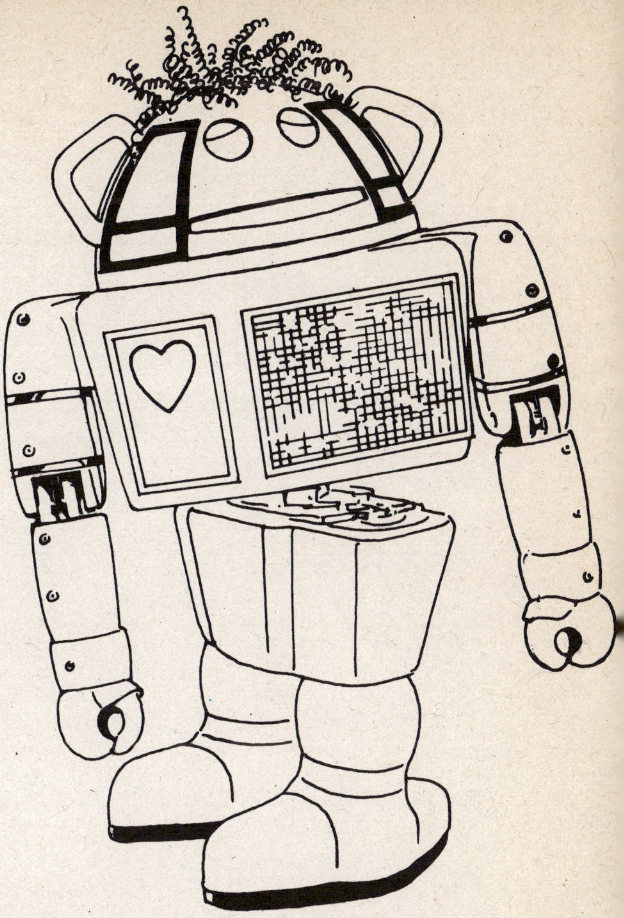

Further television appearances followed. Mickey has appeared in such shows as 'Jim'll Fix it', 'The Saturday Banana', 'Nationwide' and 'Afternoon Plus'. He is often kept busy opening department stores.

There are more Metal Mickey programmes yet to come, when we can look forward, once again, to sharing his hilarious adventures with the Wilberforce family!

Mickey has also gone into the recording business. Not only does he sing the songs, he also writes them! There appears to be no end to his talents. He loves jokes and is a great comedian!

Mickey is definitely 'on his metal' when it comes to popularity and with his many talents will be entertaining us for a long time.

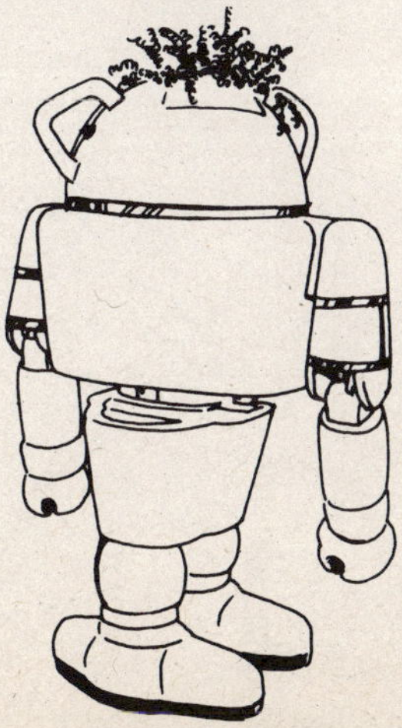

Boogie-boogie Breaker

HALEY walked into the living room. She was dressed in her best disco gear ready to go out. Metal Mickey was standing by the side of Gran's wheelchair. She was watching television. Haley gave Mickey a peck on his cheek.

"Hello my little stringbean," said Mickey.

"I sometimes wish you wouldn't call me that," replied Haley. "And anyway, I'm not so little!"

"We have noticed, my petite french bean," Mickey said mischievously. Haley pulled a face at Mickey, who pretended to look hurt. He closed his eyes, drew his ears and arms back. Haley ignored him. Mickey opened his eyes again and swivelled his head round.

"Are you going out, stringbean?" he asked.

"I'm off to the Bumble-Bee Disco," she answered.

"Wow, I'll come too, boogie-boogie."

"No you won't, you can keep Gran company," said Haley.

"Twarted again, I must be losing my sex appeal," Mickey said sadly.

"Sex appeal has nothing to do with it, I have a date!"

"I thought you said sex appeal had nothing to do with it," said Mickey, trundling after Haley, who was trying to put the finishing touches to her make-up.

"How do I look?" Haley asked Gran and Mickey.

"You use your eyes usually," replied Gran.

"I'm off now," shouted Haley, as she grabbed her coat and left the room.

"Yes," muttered Gran, "I can smell you from here!"

"Be good, Mickey," Haley called and was gone.

"I shall be superb. I only need the opportunity!" Mickey mused.

"Opportunity only knocks once," Gran said. "Switch on the telly, Fluff, there's a Fred Astair movie on."

With a little Metal Mickey magic the television came to life. The opening credits were just beginning. Gran settled back in her wheelchair to watch the film. After about half an hour Gran fell asleep. Metal Mickey wasn't in the mood for television. He fancied some excitement. He'd rather be boogieing at the disco with Haley. "Oh fiddle," he said. Mickey began to feel sorry for himself. He started to imagine all the things he could be doing. Suddenly, his audio relay condenser, fitted by Ken to improve his hearing, picked up a faint signal.

"Breaker one-four, do you copy?" said a sexy voice.

"Wow, boogie-boogie," said Metal Mickey.

The signal was from citizen band breaker Texas Rose. She picked up Metal Mickey's reply and thought 'boogie-boogie' was his handle.

"Yeh, Boogie-boogie, you've got Texas Rose, take it up to two-two."

"I'll change the dial with a smile," said Mickey. His arm lights flashed, his heart pulsated and his temperature immediately shot up to nine hundred and twenty-eight megahertz! The voice of Texas Rose was coming through loud and clear!

"Are you on channel, Boogie-boogie?"

"I'm tuned in and turned on, honey. Know what I mean, nudge, nudge, wink, wink."

"You must be close to me," said Rose, "you're bending my needle!"

Of course she means Mickey is putting out a strong signal. Before he can reply . . .

"Breaker on the side, for Texas Rose."

"We've a breaker on the side, Boogie-boogie, if you'd like to take a back seat for a moment, I'll bring him in."

"Thwarted again," sighed Mickey, "I really *must* be losing my sex-appeal!"

"Breaker on the side bring it on back," said Texas Rose.

The breaker on the side was a trucker who went under the handle 'Pigpen'.

"Yeh, you've got Pigpen here, thought I recognised your dulcet tones Texas Rose. I can't make an eyeball at the honeypot tomorrow, I've a job on and I'm going to hit the sheets early and cut some Z's. I'm taking a load of go-go girls to Crewe in the morning!"

"Greedy Pigpen," muttered Mickey.

Texas Rose told Pigpen she was sorry he wouldn't be able to make an eyeball.

"Catch you on the flip side, take care 'cause we care, breaker-break," she replied.

"I'll put the good numbers on you, breaker-break, bye-bye, I'm gone."

"Are you still on channel Boogie-boogie?

Come back."

"Wow I feel zippy again. Come back Texas Rose," said Mickey.

"Your rinky dink's modulating well, is that a four?"

"Amazomatic, no static. You're loud and clear in my ear," Mickey replied.

"Roger D on that. Are you burning rubber?" asked Texas Rose. Metal Mickey swivelled his head round and looked about the room. There didn't appear to be any signs of burning rubber.

"Can't smell anything," he said. "Unless Cleverclogs has been experimenting again!"

"Ah," said Texas Rose, "You're at your twenty."

"I'm alone with the sleeping Fruitbat. Stringbean and Stumblebum are at the Disco. Little Squirt and Cleverclogs are out. Bootface and Dippy are at the Annual Building Societies Managerial Meeting – with Potato pie supper!"

"How about an eyeball at the Honeypot Saturday?" suggested Texas Rose.

"A date, Wow," said Metal Mickey. "Okey doke and that's no joke!"

"Ten-ten 'till we do it again. On the side. Satisfied. Keep the antenna wiggling and the girls giggling. Going down, bye-bye I'm gone." said Texas Rose.

"Pretty neat huh?" said Mickey. "A date, a date!"

Mickey was making so much noise Gran woke up with a start.

"What's all the fuss, Fluff, it's only a Fred Astair film. But he is a good mover!" Mickey started to boogie about the living room. Gran clapped her hands. "Good 'ole Fluff."

"Boogie-boogie," said Mickey.

Very soon the Wilberforce household returned home. Mr Wilberforce and his wife Margery arrived first. Mr Wilberforce went straight to the conservatory to water his plants and discuss his financial affairs. He found the plants were extremely good to talk to. They never answered back. They never argued.

Mrs Wilberforce had discovered some specks of dust and promplty went to get her polish and cloths before taking her hat and coat off. It was nearly eleven o'clock, but that didn't seem to matter. She began to dust everything, including Gran, who hadn't moved from her wheelchair all evening!

Haley, Janey, Steve and Ken burst through the door laughing and giggling.

"We're all here," said Ken.

"I didn't think you were all there," replied Gran.

Haley give Mickey a peck on his cheek. "Did you miss me?" she asked.

"Not a bit," replied Mickey giving Haley one of his hurt looks. "I've got a date!"

Haley laughed. "Hey everyone, Mickey has a date!"

"Prefer figs meself," said Gran.

Mr Wilberforce was just coming out of the conservatory. He heard Haley say Mickey had a date. "If you've got a date then I'm a monkey's uncle," he said.

Mickey gave a mischievous grin. "That can be arranged," he said. His strobe lights flashed and with a little Metal Mickey magic . . . Mr Wilberforce began to prance around the room, his knees bent and his arms trailing on the floor. "Eeek, Eeek," he said. "That's the nearest thing to a monkey's uncle we'll see around here," laughed Gran.

Mr Wilberforce became himself again and couldn't understand what all the hilarity was about. "You're all crackers," he replied and went to bed. Everyone looked at Mickey. "Oh no you don't," said Ken. He, Steve and Haley dashed from the room. Janey hurriedly left for home. Only Gran stayed where she was, still in her wheelchair. "You are a card," she said to Mickey, "anyway it's time for some shut-eye, 'night Mickey."

"Night, my little Fruitbat, sweet dreams," replied Mickey.

The living room was quiet. Mickey was recharging his batteries. He closed his eyes and tried to conjour up a picture of the lovely Texas Rose. Perhaps she looks like Debbie Harrie, or Stringbean, or Kate Bush or . . . his thoughts led him to the Honeypot disco where his big date on Saturday would take place!

"Boogie-boogie," he murmured quietly and was lost in his dreams.

Saturday morning arrived and as usual the house was chaotic. Margery was frantically polishing. Bootface was in a panic. His plants

were all drooping. He couldn't understand it. He'd given them all a large dose of plant food the previous day. He checked the heating. That seemed all right. Then he checked the plant food container. "Oh no," he groaned, "what maniac did this?" He charged out of the conservatory. "Who put weed killer in the plant spray?" he demanded.

"You did, dear," said Margery. "I saw you myself."

"Why didn't you tell me?" he asked his arms flailing about. "I've murdered them all."

"Don't worry, dear, they just need a transplant," replied Margery.

"Frank Sinatra had one, so did Elton John," said Gran "and look at them now!"

Mr Wilberforce went back to the conservatory. He apologized to all the plants.

"How can you forgive me?" he said sadly, and began the task of re-potting everything in sight. He didn't reappear until tea-time!

Mickey was getting ready to go out that evening. It was only breakfast time but he wanted to look his very best. He was giving out orders to Haley and Ken.

"I need something doing to my hair," he said, looking at his reflection in the mirror. "A bit of metal polishing, an oil injection – to help me boogie better."

"Hold on," said Ken, "you're only going to a disco."

"And," said Mickey before Ken could continue, "I wouldn't mind an Atomic Thunderbuster."

"No sooner said," said Haley popping one into his mouth, ". . . than done!"

"Wow, I feel zippy, boogie-fonic, amazomatic I'm ready for off!"

"You'll blow a fuse before this evening," said Ken.

"Okey doke, Cleverclogs, but you'll be responsible!"

Ken sighed. "That robot has had a positronic brainstorm! I think we'd all better go to the disco tonight." The gang agreed. Haley, Ken, Steve and Janey would all go. There was no telling what Mickey might do, let loose on his own!

"Oh fiddle," said Mickey. "Not one chaperone but four!"

Everyone was ready for off! Mickey was in a spin. Literally! His head swivelled round, his arm lights flashed. "This is too much," he said.

Janey arrived from next door. "Where's the big night out going to be?" she asked.

"The Honeypot Disco, boogie-boogie," replied Mickey.

"Never heard of it," said Janey.

"Me neither," said Haley.

"Nor me," said Ken and Steve in unison.

"Don't panic," said Mickey. "Let's use some logic!"

"The telephone directory is a better bet," replied Haley. She flipped through the pages. "No Honeypot Disco listed here."

"PANIC!" exclaimed Mickey.

"Let's start at the very beginning," Haley suggested.

"A very good place to start," sang Gran, remembering the Sound of Music.

"What exactly did this Texas Rose say?" asked Ken.

"Well . . ." started Mickey, "she said my rinky dink was modulating well, was I burning rubber, and I was at my twenty. I didn't think I was as old as that!"

"You miserable metal maniac," muttered

Ken. "She was using citizens band code!

"That explains why the 'Honeypot' isn't listed in the directory. It's a code name for a Disco!" exclaimed Haley.

"Now all we need is to break the code and we have the meeting place!" said Janey.

"Correct!" everyone said in unison.

The gang put their heads together. Mickey began to get depressed. "Thwarted again."

"Got it," said Haley.

"Honeypot . . . Bees, Bumble Bees . . . the Bumble-Bee Disco it is."

"It is?" asked Mickey.

"It is," everyone chorused.

At last they were able to leave. Mickey was beginning to get excited again.

"Goodbye my little Fruitbat," he said to Gran.

Gran patted her eyes with a handkerchief. Mr Wilberforce grunted, "anybody would think he was going for good." Gran sobbed louder. "I hope he will be all right!"

"That *thing* is like a space invader, it's completely taking over," said Mr Wilberforce and marched through to the conservatory and the sanity of his plants.

The Bumble-Bee Disco was humming with activity. Crowds of people waited to buy their tickets, deposit their coats in the cloakroom and join in the dancing. Soon Mickey and his friends were inside. Mickey looked about him. The music was very loud, the dance floor was crowded.

"How are you going to find her in this crowd?" Haley asked Mickey.

"Er . . . did you describe yourself?" asked Ken, wondering how his metal friend *would* describe himself.

"No need, Cleverclogs, I stand out in a crowd," said Mickey.

"You can say that again," Steve murmured, looking at all the people looking at *them*.

Mickey was watching the dancing. A long legged girl with blond hair peeping from below a cream coloured 'cowboy' hat caught his eye.

"My sweet Texas Rose," he said, his strobe lights flashing.

The girl saw him and winked. Mickey moved in the direction of the dance floor.

"Wow, boogie-boogie," he said.

Haley noticed that Mickey had

disappeared. Everyone had been too busy looking for his 'date' Texas Rose. Now he, Mickey had disappeared!

"We can't lose Mickey," said Ken. "No-one could do that! He stands out in a crowd!"

"Well he's gone," concluded Haley, "we'd better split up and see if we can find him."

Steve and Ken left the girls to walk one way around the disco and they took the opposite route!

Meanwhile, Mickey introduced himself to the girl. "I am here for the eyeball, boogie-boogie," he said.

Texas Rose smiled. "You are not quite what I expected," she said.

"Pretty neat, huh?" replied Mickey.

"You could say that!" exclaimed Rose.

"Let's boogie," said Mickey, and joined the other dancers on the crowded dance floor.

The crowd of dancers dispersed to watch Metal Mickey and Texas Rose boogieing! They were a sensation. Everyone cheered! Ken and Steve groaned when they saw Mickey.

"He's making an exhibition of himself," said Ken. "C'mon, let's rescue the girl."

Haley and Janey joined the boys. Mickey was causing quite a stir!

"Is this er . . ." said Ken looking for a suitable word to describe Mickey.

"Is *he* troubling you?" he finished lamely.

"Not at all," replied Texas Rose, "I've never had so much fun in ages! Come on everybody, boogie with Boogie-boogie!"

"Mickey," said Metal Mickey.

"Okay Mickey, let's hit it."

Everyone joined in the dancing. Mickey was a 'hit'. The dancers cheered him on.

When it was time to go home, Texas Rose gave Mickey a big kiss and a little tummy rub!

"Wow," said Mickey.

"Put your ears on tomorrow and I'll talk to you then," said Texas Rose.

"Okey-doke, ten-ten 'till we do it again!" Mickey replied giving her a wink.

"He's got it bad," said Haley.

"I'd say, I've got it good, good buddies," replied Mickey enjoying the C.B. lingo.

"Is that a four?" he added mischievously, swivelling his head and flashing all his lights.

"Roger D, going down . . . !"

C.B. CODE-BREAKER

Metal Mickey has mastered the Citizens Band code. He had decided to let you know some of the lingo. So put your ears on.....!

Breaker	C.B. User
one-four	Call channel
do you copy?	Are you receiving?
take it up	Move to another channel
bending my needle	Strong signal
breaker on the side	another person wishing to speak
take a back seat	wait a moment
bring it on back	start talking
handle	code name
eyeball	meeting
hit the sheets, cut some Z's	go to bed
go-go girls	pigs
flip side	return trip
breaker-break	sign off
put the good numbers on you	sign off
rinky dink	C.B. radio
modulating	talking
is that a four?	is that right?
Roger D	message received
burning rubber	driving vehicle, mobile
twenty	home
ten ten till we do it again	sign off
on the side, satisfied	,,
keep the antenna wiggling and the girls giggling	,,
going down	,,
boogieing	party going
put your ears on	listen

mickey's metropolis

1

2

3

4

5

6

7

8

9

10

The pictures on this page, are of famous buildings, monuments and places to be seen in London. Mickey is only showing part of the picture. He wants you to see if you can recognise them. Do you know what they are, and where in London they can be found. The answers and complete pictures are on pages 78 and 79, the back end papers.

SNOWMAN MICKEY

1. Mickey was standing by the window watching the snow fall. "Pretty neat fluff stuff," he said. Gran was in her wheelchair surrounded by pillows, rugs and two hot water bottles. She hates the snow, it's cold, damp and makes her bones ache and her feet feel like lead.

2. Mickey decided to go outside. He opened the front door and the snow from the roof fell down on top of him! He didn't know that snow would make him rust. His arms started to seize up. Mickey groaned. He couldn't move. "This is the end," he said to himself.

3. Two children were playing in the snow. They spotted 'Snowman Mickey' and ran over to him. Mickey asked them to bring him a hot water bottle. The children laughed, threw a snowball at him and ran off. "It's no use, it's definitely the end," he sighed.

4. Gran noticed that Mickey had disappeared and searched the house for him. He was nowhere to be found! She opened the front door and peeped outside. "Flippin' kids," she said, "leavin' that thing there!" "Hello my little Fruitbat," said Mickey. "I'm rusting, it's the end."

5. "Goodness, it really is you, Fluff," said Gran, forgetting about the cold and struggling to get Mickey inside. She stood him against the radiator, wrapped him in his scarf and hat and went off to get a hot water bottle to help to thaw him out.

6. Mickey's arms creaked and his head made a horrible grating noise when he tried to move it. Gran had an idea. She dashed to the garage and came back to Mickey, carrying an oil can. She began to squirt oil all over Mickey's creaking joints!

7. "Eureka!" shouted Mickey. Gran told him not to be cheeky, she had showered that morning! Soon Mickey was his normal self and felt much better. He and Gran played a few games of 'snap' to pass the time. The Wilberforce family would be home from work soon.

8. Later that evening, Haley was sitting at the table cleaning her face with cotton wool and cleansing lotion. Mickey looked at the cotton wool. It was most interesting. "Fluff stuff," he mused, "and it isn't wet." He emanated, his strobe lights flashed and a low tone sounded.

9. Mickey's magic powers were at work! Outside the snow continued to fall but it wasn't wet. It wouldn't make him rust. The snow was small balls of cotton wool and it was getting thicker and thicker! Mickey went to the window to watch. "Lovely, fluff stuff," he said softly.

10. Next day, the cotton wool snow was almost two feet deep. Cotton wool icebergs were floating down the river Thames! London was virtually at a standstill. Experts were called in to give advice, but everyone was baffled by this mysterious phenomenon.

11. Gran was watching television. There was a 'newsflash'. "The army has been called out to move this peculiar snow that threatens our city..." Gran pulled a face. "Everlasting snow, whatever next!" she said. "It's all them rockets, you know, does something to the atmosphere!"

12. Mr. Wilberforce came into the living room. He was wearing a red 'Santa' costume. He'd been roped in to play Father Christmas at a local store but he couldn't find his beard. He asked Margery if she had seen it. Margery was dusting, as usual and gave him an odd look.

13. She told her husband, the beard was where it usually was — in the washbasin and if he needed it he'd better hurry up because she was going to clean up and it would be washed away. Mr. Wilberforce sighed. His wife always misunderstood him!

14. Eventually, Mr. Wilberforce made his wife understand that it was his cotton wool beard that was lost. "Oh dear," sighed Margery, "it's in the garage." He charged out to get it but when he opened the door all he could see were several poly bags.

15. "What's this? Oh no, bags full of fluff stuff! Well it must be here somewhere," he muttered tipping the contents of the bags onto the path. He foraged through the cotton wool trying to find his beard. He would have to hurry up or he would be late on his first day!

16. At last he found it and was ready for off. He hurriedly said goodbye to Margery and was gone. Gran saw the cotton wool on the path and let out an almighty shriek, "there's an iceberg on the path!" "Now how did I miss that?" asked Margery, who was convinced she moved it all.

17. Gran and Mickey were alone. "Can you keep a secret, my little Fruitbat?" said Mickey. "Cross me heart and hope to die," replied Gran. Mickey told her that he was responsible for the fluff stuff. "How could you?" asked Gran. But really it was simple. A little Mickey magic made it!

18. Mickey decided to go for a walk. This time, he wouldn't rust. His magic snow was rustproof! As he walked along the cotton wool snow clung to him. "Lovely fluff stuff," he said. "I make a pretty neat snowman, boogie-boogie."

19. There didn't seem to be many people about and Mickey plodded through the snow laden streets. Now and again he stopped to look at the brightly decorated shops. It would soon be Christmas. There would be lots of presents, Christmas crackers and decorations. It would be great fun!

20. Mickey stopped at a large department store in the high street. The window was brightly decorated with coloured lights. Mr. Wilberforce was seated in the Christmas Grotto at the far end of the store. Snowman Mickey decided to go in. Bootface was in for a few surprises!

continued on page 38

MIRROR

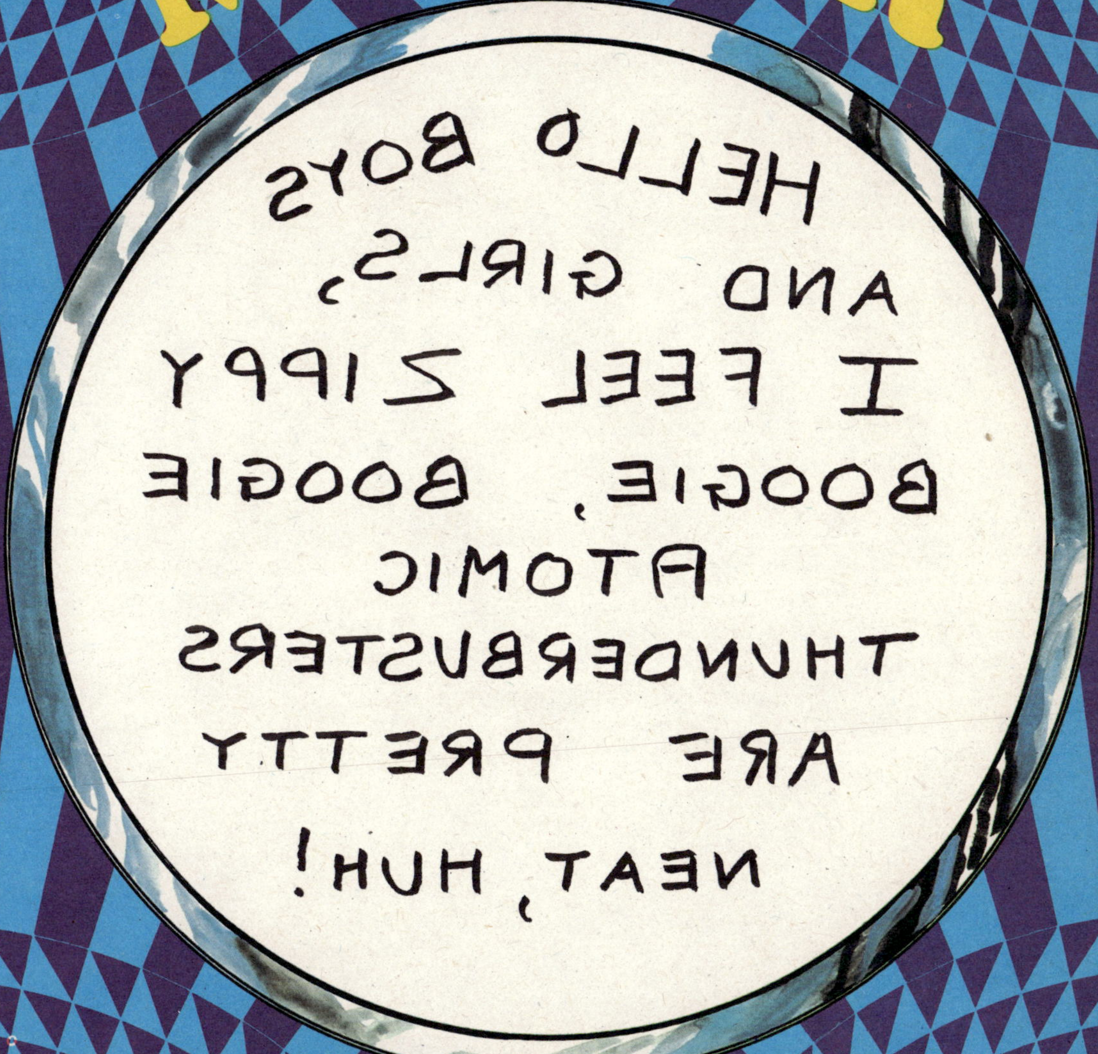

IMAGE

If you hold the card in front of a mirror you can read Metal Mickey's message!

Mickey takes a joke!

Joke: Which pop group does Metal Mickey like best?
Ans. Tin Lizzy!

Joke: How does Metal Mickey stand?
Ans. Bolt upright!

Joke: How will Metal Mickey be married?
Ans. At a simple welding ceremony!

Joke: Does Metal Mickey have any brothers?
Ans. No. Just tran-sisters!

Joke: Why did Metal Mickey go to the doctor?
Ans. Because he had metal fatigue!

Joke: What is Metal Mickey's theme song?
Ans. My Oil Can-tucky Home!

Joke: Who is Metal Mickey's favourite comedian?
Ans. Cosmis Smallpiece!

Joke: What girls does Metal Mickey like best?
Ans. Platinum blondes!

Joke: Who is Metal Mickey's favourite film star?
Ans. Dustbin Hoffman.

Joke: Why did Metal Mickey go to the dentist?
Ans. To have metal filings in his teeth!

Joke: Where does Metal Mickey wash?
Ans. In the zinc!

Joke: Who is Metal Mickey's favourite dog?
Ans. Rin Tin Tin

Mickey and the GREEN ROBOT

IT WAS just after midnight. All the Wilberforce family were asleep in bed, each in their own dreams!

Gran was dreaming about an Arabian knight in the shape of Rudolf Valentino (WHO?). He was whisking her away on the back of a white horse, to his tent, where he brought her Turkish Delight on a velvet cushion!

Mr. Wilberforce was having so much success with his plants it was almost unbelievable. He was up to his neck in compost and triffids! He managed to sell the triffids forty-nine percent of the shares in his building society – even though he's only the manager! By keeping fifty-one percent controlling interest, what could have been a nightmare, was turning out to be one of his quieter nights sleep!

Ken was in Frankenstein's laboratory. The famed professor was about to bring his monster to life. With the help of Ken's super technological mind and total incapacity to get things quite right, the experiment was moving very slowly.

Mrs. Wilberforce was in her element cleaning Buckingham Palace in time for a visit from a foreign president!

Steve was too tired to dream!

Haley was receiving proposals from Clint Eastwood, Robert Redford and several other famous stars of the silver screen. Her Father was telling her they were all too old – and what were they proposing anyway!? It was all so confusing. She would be glad when it was time to get up!

Downstairs in the living room, Mickey was re-charging his batteries. He was dreaming about 'Blondie'. She was just about to give him a tummy rub, when a funny thing happened! His arm lights flashed involuntarily and a tingling sensation ran through him! He thought it was the anticipation of a tummy rub. It happened again! He wasn't dreaming at all!

He opened his eyes. "Is anybody there?" he asked, sounding like a medium at a seance. He swivelled his head round. Everything looked all right. But it didn't feel all right! Suddenly, an illuminous purple orb appeared before him. A strange looking Green Robot stepped from the orb, which then disappeared. The Robot moved towards Mickey. It was a bright emerald green colour with two large, black eyes set into a dome-shaped head. It had a peculiar spiked aerial sticking out of the top.

"You are a humanoid?" the Green Robot asked Mickey.

"I am?" queried Mickey.

"Affirmative," replied the Green Robot.

Mickey dis-engaged himself from his batteries and approached the Robot. He asked him if he wasn't feeling very well. He was a very funny colour! The Robot, looking at Mickey, was about to ask him the same!

"Humanoids are inferior species," the Robot uttered.

"Not at all. They're pretty neat," said Mickey, thinking of Debbie Harrie, Haley, Fruitbat, Mr. Wilberforce . . .! Except Bootface, even *he* thinks he's inferior! But he does have green fingers."

"Ah," said the Green Robot, "he must be responding to the Kranian super-ray. He would make a good specimen for research!"

"So the psychiatrist thinks!" exclaimed Mickey.

"Where is this Bootface?" asked the Green Robot.

"In the land of nod I expect," came the reply.

"The land of nod is not listed in my schedule," said the Robot, "you will have to do."

"Do what, Mush?" asked Mickey.

"Come with me."

"The pleasure is all yours, but we haven't been introduced," said Mickey.

"I come from Krania, my name is Spectra," replied the Robot.

Mickey thought the name sounded like the Russian agents in the Bond films. "A bit like James Bond," he commented.

"Pleased to meet you, James Bond," said Spectra.

"Is he here too?" Mickey said, swivelling his head round.

"Ah!" exclaimed the Robot, "you have mastered more than we supposed." Spectra was watching Metal Mickey's spinning head. It was very interesting. His superiors would be pleased with this specimen.

"We had better leave now," Spectra emphasised, "there is much to do!"

"Okey-doke," said Mickey, "but what about Bootface?"

"The land of nod is not on my schedule," repeated the Robot.

"Leave this to me," said Mickey, closing his eyes and concentrating. Mickey's super powers began to work. The sleeping Mr. Wilberforce levitated from his bed and slowly moved towards the bedroom door. 'Click', the bedroom door opened. Mr. Wilberforce floated through. He glided down the stairs, tugging at invisible sheets and curling up. He appeared to be feeling the cold night air. The living room door opened and Mr. Wilberforce drifted in.

"There," said Mickey, "meet Bootface."

Mr. Wilberforce was still fast asleep. He floated on the air, oblivious to everything!

Spectra went nearer. He wanted a closer

look at this Bootface! Mr. Wilberforce was wearing blue striped pyjamas. The Robot touched the fabric. "Ugh," he said with disgust, "this Bootface has a strange covering, blue stripes and pink bits sticking out of every corner. It will probably wear out very quickly!"

Mickey agreed and pointed to a small cut on Mr. Wilberforce's finger.

"They damage easily," he said.

Spectra looked at the cut finger. It had been bleeding and was still very red. "All the stuffing is coming out of this machine," said the Robot, "it is indeed – *most* inferior!"

Spectra's mission to collect specimens of earthlings was now complete. They were ready to return to Krania. He hoped his superiors would approve of his choice! The purple orb re-appeared, Metal Mickey, Spectra and the floating Mr. Wilberforce went inside. They were on their way to Krania. In an instant the orb had vanished and the living room was silent.

There was a welcoming committee awaiting them as the orb touched down on Krania. Metal Mickey stepped out first and trundled across to the Kranians, who all looked very much like his new friend Spectra.

"Greetings earthling," said the Kranian Ambassador.

"Boogie-boogie, it's an amazomatic planet, everything's green or purple," said Mickey, surveying the rocky green and purple hillside.

Mickey levitated Mr. Wilberforce from out of the purple orb. Spectra followed. They all went to the Kranian laboratory, Mr. Wilberforce floating alongside. Once inside, the Kranian Ambassador pointed to what looked like an operating table. Several powerful lights shone down on the area. "We will put the specimen there," said the Ambassador. Mr. Wilberforce was placed on the table. The Kranians gathered round him. Mickey watched with great interest as the Kranians huddled together around Bootface, who was completely oblivious to their mutterings.

The Kranians took X-rays of Mr. Wilberforce. They were very shocked to see what was inside! Perhaps they should remove a few parts to see how they worked?

"That's not a good idea, Mush," said Mickey who had been looking on. "Once the 'stuffing' is taken out of him, it's difficult to put it back in the right order," said Mickey. "It could malfunction!" he added.

"Not a good specimen at all," sighed Spectra. "Perhaps we could send him on our forthcoming inter-galactic mission. In five thousand years he would return to Krania and we could continue the experiment!"

"Definitely not a good idea, Mush," replied Mickey. "The parts wear out long before that!"

The Kranians were very puzzled. This Bootface was indeed an inferior humanoid! The only solution was to feed him into the Sonic Inversion Ray Detector – Sird for short! Mr. Wilberforce was wheeled over to the machine. In he went! Everyone waited by the exit hatch and computer read-out. The conveyor belt clicked into action and a transformed Mr. Wilberforce came through the exit. Mickey and the Kranians surveyed the changes. Mickey did not appear too perturbed by a strange looking green blob wearing blue striped pyjamas!

"Definitely vegetable matter," said Spectra. "The computer read-out states, 80% water content, some trace elements, minerals and chemicals. A low intelligence form of plant, I'd say," he concluded.

Mickey explored the laboratory. At the far end, a machine lay idle. He looked closely at it. "What's this?" he asked Spectra.

"Climp," replied the Green Robot.

Mickey was not amused. He levitated Spectra and threatened to send him floating away forever.

"I mean, it's the Cosmic Linear Infra Magnetic Pulsator – Climp for short," retorted the Green Robat.

"Okey, doke, Mush! How does it work?"

"I don't know, no-one on Krania knows," replied Spectra.

Mickey released the Robot from his powers and went to talk to the Climp machine. The computer activated. It took thirty seconds for a complete read-out. Mickey set to work. The Kranians watched with fascination as the green blob was transferred to the Climp machine. Mickey pressed switches, pulled levers and finally put the green blob inside. Green and purple lights flashed and in an instant Mr. Wilberforce popped out of the machine. He was himself again, and this time wideawake!

"Where am I?" he gasped. "I feel most peculiar."

Mickey didn't get the opportunity to reply. Spectra and the other Green Robots were all talking at once! Mickey was their hero!

"You have made history on Krania. Long ago our Masters made the Climp machine. It was invaluable to our planet. After the eclipse of the dwarf red sun our Masters perished and the machine has been idle ever since that time. We no longer need earthling specimens for our research. Climp will solve all our problems. Our thanks oh one of much genius! You can have anything you ask. Whatever we have is yours, except the Climp machine, of course!"

"Of course," replied Mickey, with great dignity. "My only wish is to borrow the purple orb and take Bootface back to the land of nod." The Kranians glanced in the direction of Mr. Wilberforce. He appeared to be talking to himself, muttering something like 'metallic monstrosities."

"Is that all you desire?" asked Spectra.

"I wouldn't mind an Atomic Thunderbuster!"

Spectra pressed several switches on the Sird machine – Atomic Thunderbusters flew out in every direction!

"Wow, boogie-boogie, that's pretty neat," said Mickey popping one into his mouth.

It was time to leave. With great ceremony, Mickey was presented with the Kranian medal for Technical Achievement in Scientific

Research. The Ambassador put it round Mickey's neck. Like everything else on Krania, it was purple and the lettering 'T.A.S.R.' was in green.

"Goodbye my earthling friend," said Spectra.

The purple orb re-appeared and Mickey and Mr. Wilberforce stepped inside. In no time at all they were back in the living room. Mr. Wilberforce was still in a dream-like daze.

"Okey-doke, Bootface, back to the land of nod," said Mickey.

As if in an hypnotic trance, Mr. Wilberforce went back to bed. Mickey was feeling tired, it was time to re-charge his batteries. He touched the purple disc around his neck. He had enjoyed his visit to Krania.

Next day at breakfast, Mr. Wilberforce was looking rather green! He didn't feel well and was glad it was Saturday and he didn't have to go to the office.

"I feel like a jelly," he said shakily.

"Lime flavoured, by the look of you," replied Gran.

"It was those green robots," he said, wondering what on earth he was talking about.

"Yes dear," said Margery. Perhaps you had better see a doctor!"

"Doctor? What?", he asked angrily.

"It's Doctor Who!" replied Gran, and he's not on the telly until ten past five!"

Mickey asked Gran if she would play a game of snap or dominoes with him. Mr. Wilberforce noticed the medal around Mickey's neck.

"I'm going out," he said to Mickey, "you are driving me round the bend. You are responsible for all that has happened."

"And I got a medal for it!" exclaimed Mickey, winking at Gran.

"What you been up to, Fluff?" asked Gran.

"Me?" asked Mickey, "nothing at all really. I feel adventurous, how about doubling the stakes?

Gran began to deal the cards. "You're on," she said, "set up the Atomic Thunderbusters!"

To make spinner –

Trace and copy onto thin card. Colour with felt pens and put on the numbers. Push a cocktail stick (or matchstick) through the centre.

MISS A GO. MAKE GRAN A CUP OF TEA

ATOMIC THUNDER BUSTER

HAVE TWO GOES

Metal Mickey's atomic THUNDER-BUSTER Game

LOSE WAY GO BACK THREE SQUARES

A game for two or more players.

You need dice or spinner, a button or counter for each player. 6 buttons (these are the Thunderbusters) keep on one side. When a player lands on a square containing a Thunderbuster he picks up one button. You can only carry one button round the board! The First player to pick up THREE Thunderbusters and put them in Mickey's basket wins the game!

ATOMIC THUNDER BUSTER

SNOWMAN MICKEY (PART TWO)

1. Mr. Wilberforce made a splendid Father Christmas. He was sitting in a sleigh with two large plastic reindeers at the front. Snowman Mickey covered from head to foot in fluff stuff, looked like part of the glittering setting.

2. Mr. Wilberforce asked a little girl what she would like Santa to bring her for Christmas. At the sight of his long white beard, she let out an almighty wail and began to scream with fright. Metal Mickey giggled as Mr. Wilberforce tried to console her!

3. The queue of children waiting to see Santa, grew and grew. One little boy showed a lot of interest in the snowman. He thought Mickey was much better than the decrepit old Santa. When Mickey heard the comments, he started to giggle again. He was enjoying himself!

4. Snowman Mickey stole the show. He was a sensation! "Pretty neat,huh?" he said, "I'm the star of the Christmas Grotto!" One of the children heard Mickey speak and started to prance around shouting, "the snowman spoke to me, he's real. Yippee!"

5. Soon all the children had gathered around Mickey. They thought he was fantastic. "Boogie-boogie," said Mickey. Poor Mr. Wilberforce felt downcast. He wondered what was attracting the children's attention and went to investigate. "Oh! No! Not Mickey, it can't be?" he gasped.

6. But it was! "Hello Bootface Santa. It's me, Snowman Mickey. What would you like for Christmas?" asked Mickey. "You-you scene stealer," stammered Mr. Wilberforce, "the children came to see me, not a tin pot snowman!"

7. "We want the snowman, we want the snowman," chanted the children. Mr. Wilberforce walked back to his sleigh. His first day in the Christmas Grotto was ruined and it was all Mickey's fault. Mickey had an idea. He would cheer up Bootface!

8. With a little Metal Mickey magic, Mr. Wilberforce and his sleigh and reindeers took to the air. "See Santa fly," shouted Mickey. The children cheered. Mr. Wilberforce began to feel dizzy. "Steady Rudolf," he shrieked frantically pulling the reins!

9. The sleigh was out of control. The parcels cascaded down. "Yippee," shouted the children, "presents from Santa!" Everyone scrabbled to pick up the parcels. Christmas decorations began to fall as Mr. Wilberforce fought to control the reindeers!

10. "Help", shouted Mr. Wilberforce. "Snowman Mickey to the rescue!" exclaimed Mickey, bringing the sleigh down to the ground with a bump! The Grotto was devastated. A stern faced manager approached Mr. Wilberforce. "You're fired!" he said.

11. Mr. Wilberforce left in a hurry. He'd suffered enough humiliation. Mickey looked at the mess. With a final touch of magic, the Grotto was restored and Mickey decided to go home. The children were sad to see him leave and waved and shouted.

12. It was still snowing outside. Mickey walked very slowly through the thick cotton wool snow. All around him people were trying in vain to get rid of it. They shovelled it into bags and bins but as fast as they moved it, the fluff stuff piled up again.

13. Mickey arrived home at last. Gran was still watching television. He went over to her. "Hello, my little Fruitbat," he said. "Look at this," sniffed Gran, dabbing her eyes with a handkerchief. "That poor, poor man, we must do something!"

14. Mickey watched the television programme for a few minutes. Suddenly he became very excited. His arm lights flashed on and off. "We can help," he exclaimed. "We can?" asked Gran. "Yes", replied Mickey, "Super Gran and Mickey to the rescue!"

15. It appeared that a local toy manufacturer was about to go out of business because he could not find anyone to supply the filling for his gigantic fluffy toys. Mickey's idea was simple. The fluff stuff was ideal. It was soft, white and virtually indestructible!

16. Gran listened to Mickey's plan. She was delighted. They would go to the factory at once. They had to walk very slowly through the thick snow. When they arrived, Gran was feeling very tired. "Goodness!" she exclaimed, "I'm out of puff and me legs are giving me gyp!"

17. Mr. Royale was the owner of Royale-T-Toys. Gran and Mickey were shown into his office. They told him of their plan to save the factory. Mr. Royale beamed. Why hadn't he thought of it? The factory could now stay in business. Everyone would have a happy Christmas!

18. Mickey had triumphed again. "It was nothing really, Mush," he said winking at Gran. "The fluff stuff wasn't very popular. People seem to prefer real snow!" Mr. Royale laughed. He showed Gran and Mickey around the workshops.

19. Mickey pointed to a large pink elephant. "That is just the thing for Haley, she'd love it!" Mr. Royale overheard and told Mickey he could have the elephant. "Boogie-boogie, that's pretty neat, huh?" said Mickey. Gran agreed. "It's smashing," she said.

20. Gran, Mickey and the pink elephant were taken home in Mr. Royale's Rolls Royce. Haley was thrilled with her present. Mickey went over to the window. It was time to turn the fluff stuff back to real snow. He would have to stay in until it melted. But he had Christmas to look forward to!

COSMIC ZONE MAZE

Travel through the Cosmic Zone maze and take Mickey to his Atomic Thunderbusters.

ER

ER

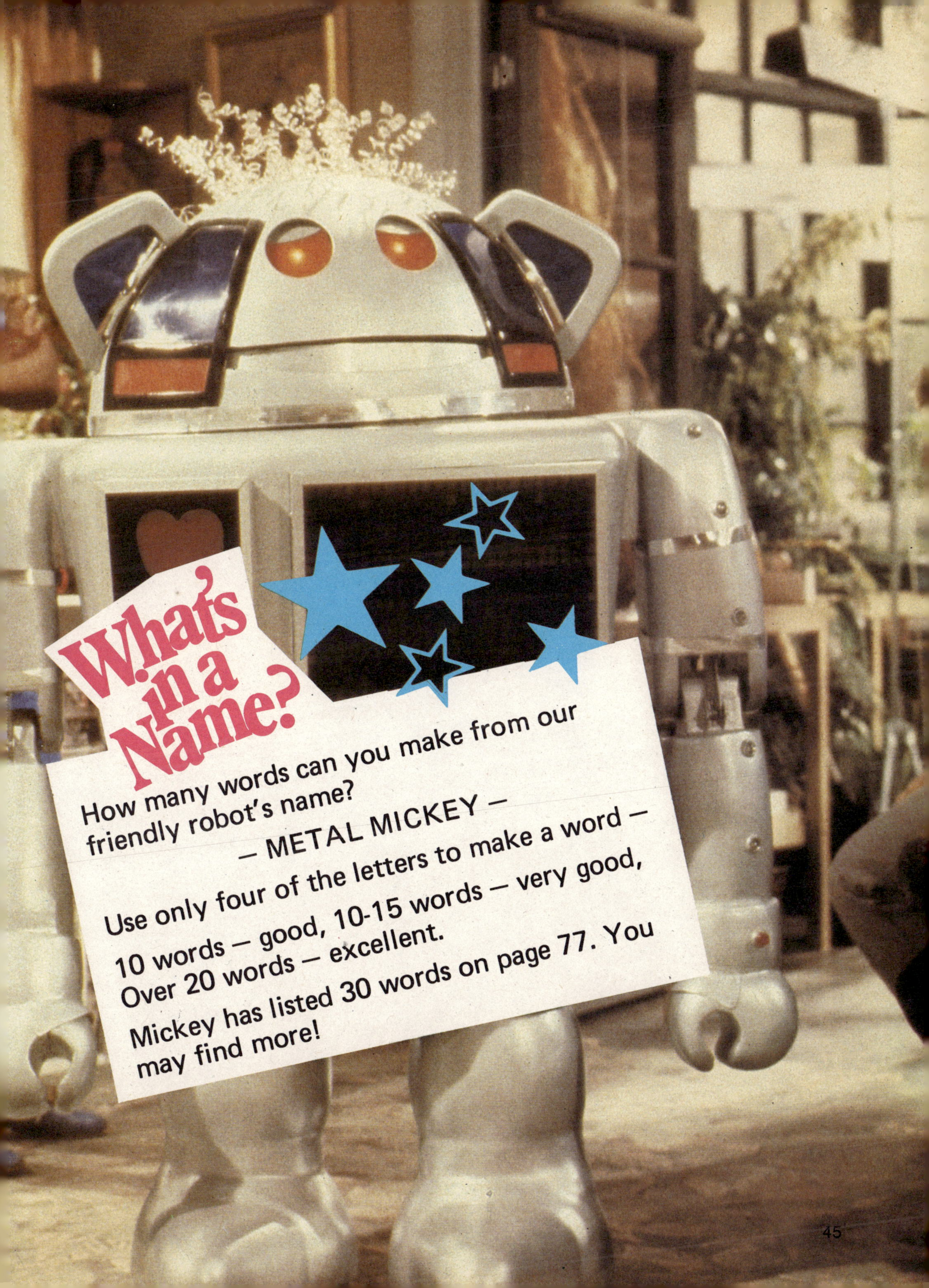

What's in a Name?

How many words can you make from our friendly robot's name?

— METAL MICKEY —

Use only four of the letters to make a word — 10 words — good, 10-15 words — very good, Over 20 words — excellent.

Mickey has listed 30 words on page 77. You may find more!

Caring for plants the Wilberforce way

When Mr. Wilberforce isn't working at the building society office, he spends most of his time caring for his plants. He considers himself to be what could be called an expert on the subject. He has listed the do's and don'ts of perfect plant care. How to transplant your plants or alternatively take cuttings from them. How to water and feed your plants and avoid the ginger tom from next door doing it for you. How to keep your plants pest free. He is exceptionally well experienced in this, having lived with Metal Mickey for some considerable time. The right container for the right plants. Grannies chamber pot is a good idea provided you don't take it from under the bed. Someone might miss it! Especially Grannie!

If you are adept at growing from seeds you will need a very shallow tray. But is is advisable not to use the one from the bottom of the budgies cage!

Bulbs, especially not the electric kind, are nice to cultivate and make lovely presents for family and friends. After planting the bulbs, they must be kept in a dark place until the first green shoots appear. They can then be brought into a light, airy, warm place.

Mr. Wilberforce firmly believes in talking to flowers and plants. They respond to a kind word now and again. A lot of noise, shouting

or arguing can cause the plants to feel unwanted, whereupon they are liable to wilt, droop or even, (don't read this out aloud) fade away completely!

All devoted plant lovers will be aware of how a little love and kindness towards plants makes them thrive and flourish. And don't forget even prickly cacti like a kind word now and again. It's particularly advisable to talk to the very prickly variety when re-potting or watering as they are liable to leave one of their nasty prickly bits in you! By the way cacti are used to dry climates and don't like a lot of water, so go easy on the H_2O. If that highly technical bit of information baffled any of you — H_2O is water.

Holiday time! Ah, you might ask, and well you might — do plants go on holiday? Well of course that is total nonsense. Or is it? Do you cheerfully pack all your bags and belongings, put a note out for the milkman, cancel the newspapers, send the cat to the cattery and think — "that's it? " You may be very conscientious and turn off all the electricity at the mains and also turn off the water in case of burst pipes. That's definitely it? Not so. What about the plants? Well what about them you ask? Don't you? Then why are you reading about caring for plants if not? The best advice, Wilberforce style, is find your plants a good home for the length of time you will be away. Yes! A holiday for your plants! New horizons, fresh people, different coloured wallpaper to gaze upon. You will find that when you return home suffering from blisters, sunburn, dysentry and food poisoning, your plants are happy, healthy and literally blooming.

Now if you are still looking for the list of do's and don'ts, then don't. Mr. Wilberforce has decided not to write one. All the information is contained here. Sift through it until you are all word perfect then go away and practise on the real thing. With dedication you too can perfect the Wilberforce method of caring for plants. Good luck! Have a blooming good time as well. 'Bye, until the next exciting feature.

INSTANT WIT!

WHAT TREE IS LIKE A COAT?

WHAT ALWAYS WEIGHS THE SAME, NO MATTER WHAT SIZE IT IS?

WHY ARE GRANNIES LIKE EXPENSIVE FISH?

WHY IS THE LETTER 'G' LIKE THE SUN?

WHAT ALWAYS HAS ITS HEART IN ITS HEAD?

WHICH WEIGHS MORE, A FULL MOON OR A QUARTER MOON?

WHAT HAS MANY TEETH BUT CAN'T EAT?

WHY DOES THE COFFEE TASTE LIKE MUD?

WHICH 4 LETTERS OF THE ALPHABET DESCRIBE AN EMPTY HORSE?

FIR.
A HOLE!
THEY'RE DEAR OLE SOLES!
BECAUSE IT'S THE CENTRE OF 'LIGHT'.
LETTUCE.
A FULL MOON IS LIGHTER.
A COMB.
BECAUSE IT WAS 'GROUND' THIS MORNING!
M.T.G.G.

MICKEY'S got a CODE in the head!

Using his code diagram, decipher the message!

With Mickey's code you can make your own secret messages to send to your buddies, and, with a little of Mickey's genius you can make up your own code.

A	B	C	D	E	F	G	H	I	J	K	L	M	N	O	P	Q	R	S	T	U	V	W	X	Y	Z
N	O	P	Q	R	S	T	U	V	W	X	Y	Z	A	B	C	D	E	F	G	H	I	J	K	L	M

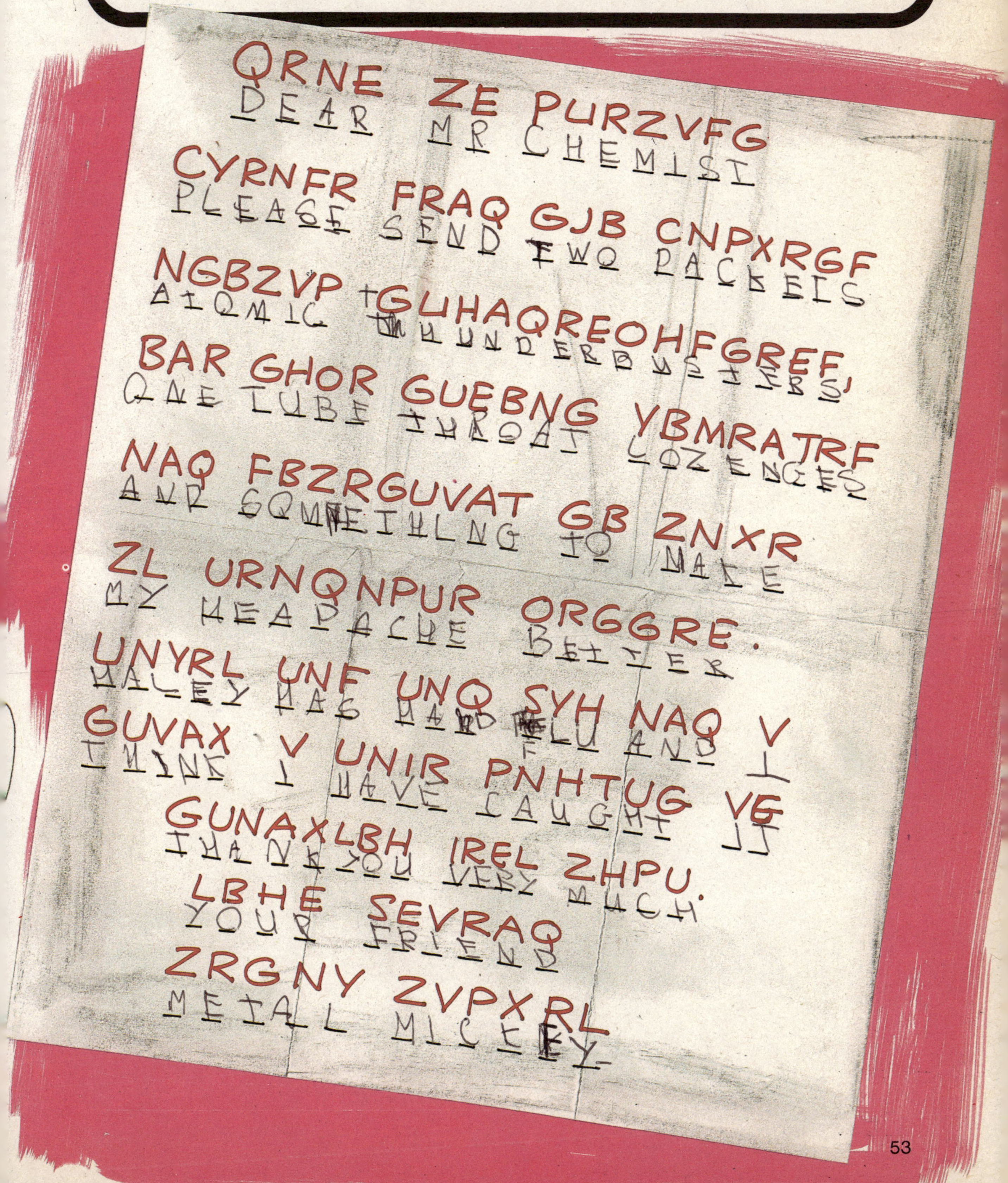
QRNE ZE PURZVFG
DEAR MR CHEMIST
CYRNFR FRAQ GJB CNPXRGF
PLEASE SEND TWO PACKETS
NGBZVP GUHAQREOHFGREF
ATOMIC THUNDERBUSTERS
BAR GHOR GUEBNG YBMRATRF
ONE TUBE THROAT LOZENGES
NAQ FBZRGUVAT GB ZNXR
AND SOMETHING TO MAKE
ZL URNQNPUR ORGGRE.
MY HEADACHE BETTER
UNYRL UNF UNQ SYH NAQ V
HALEY HAS HAD FLU AND I
GUVAX V UNIR PNHTUG VG
THINK I HAVE CAUGHT IT
GUNAXLBH IREL ZHPU.
THANK YOU VERY MUCH
LBHE SEVRAQ
YOUR FRIEND
ZRGNY ZVPXRL
METAL MICKEY

‘go on-go back’

Directions.

1. You will need a coin for each player to use as a marker and one pencil.
2. With your eyes tightly shut, place the pencil point into the box below with the numbers **1-2-3.**
3. Wherever your pencil point lands – this is the number of moves you can make.
4. If a player lands on a circle occupied by another player – he must wait in the circle before that one, until his next turn.
5. There are some ‘Go On’ and ‘Go Back’ circles. If you land on these, follow the arrow directions.
6. The player reaching Mickey first is declared **the winner.**

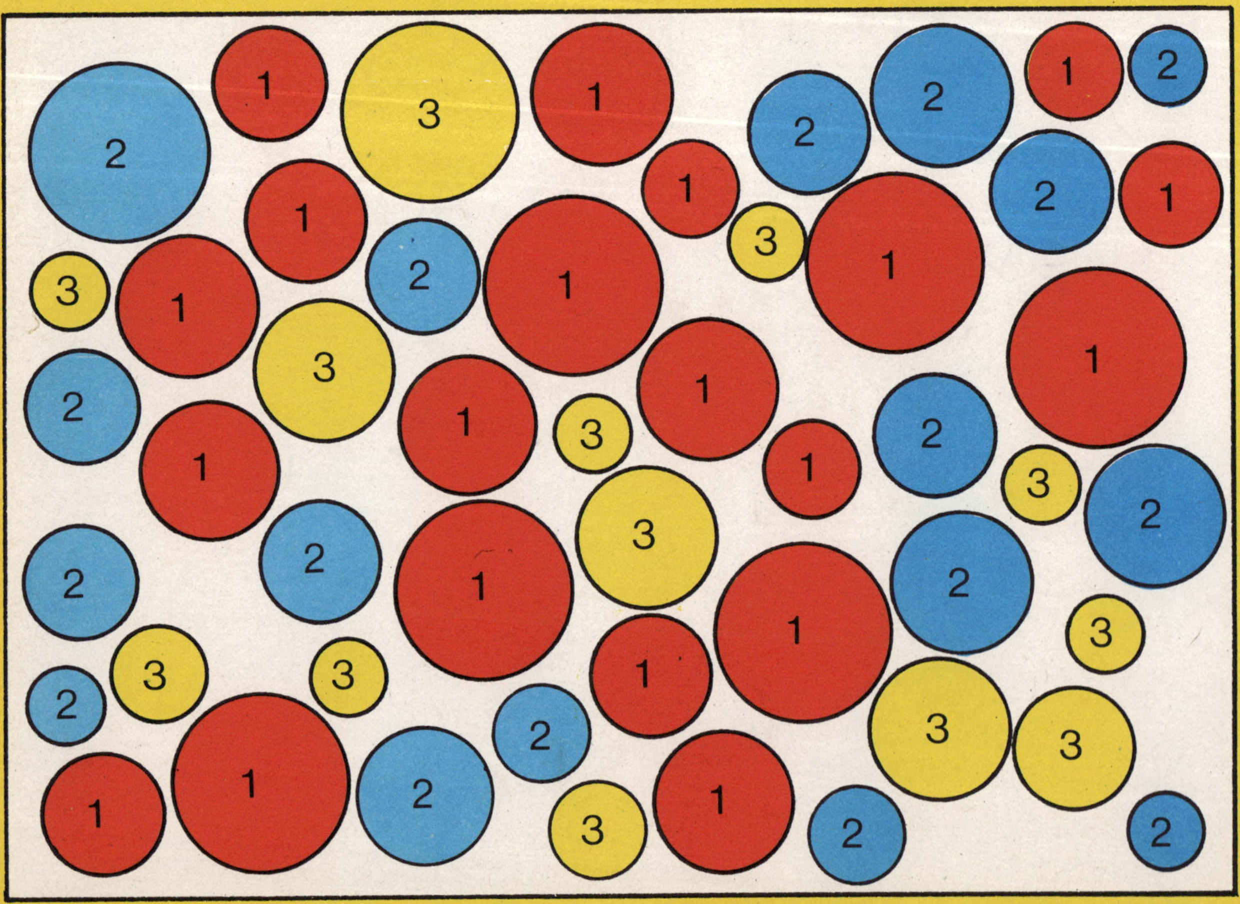

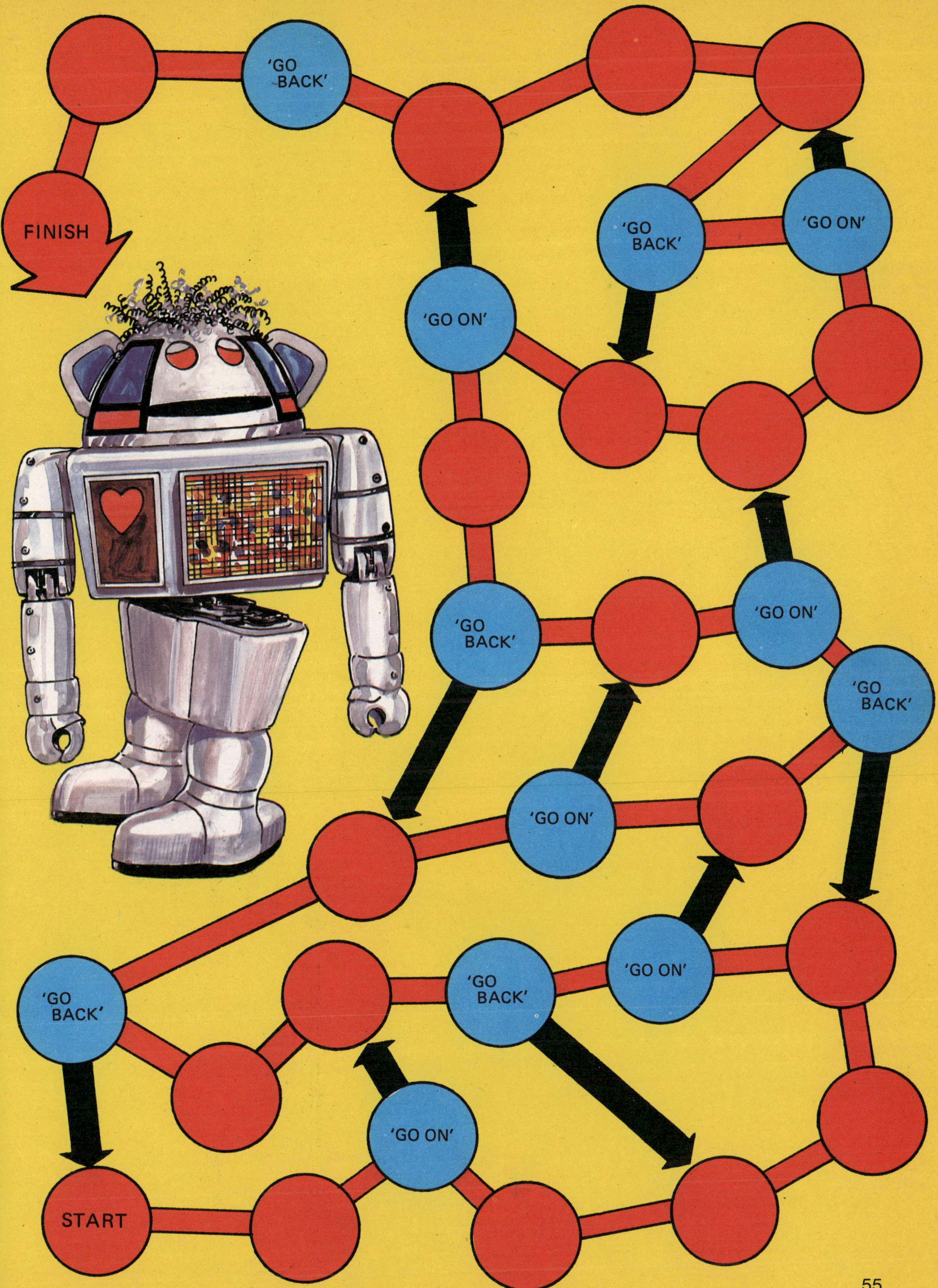
FINISH
'GO BACK'
'GO BACK'
'GO ON'
'GO ON'
'GO BACK'
'GO ON'
'GO BACK'
'GO ON'
'GO BACK'
'GO ON'
'GO BACK'
'GO ON'
START

METAL MICKEY'S CROSSWORD

Clueless crosswords are for people who haven't a clue! This one has ten clues! Remember it's been divised by the mischievous Metal Mickey. Study the clues carefully... you have been warned... Have fun! If you find the puzzle too difficult, Mickey has given the answers on page 77.

Clues Across.

1. An alcoholic fruit drink served at parties.
6. A famous satirical magazine.
7. A blow with the fist.
8. An engineering tool, used to make holes.
9. The leading character in puppet show. Married to Judy.

1 P	2 EU	3 N	4 C	5 H
6	W			
7 UP	EU	N	C	H
8 D	R	I	L	L
9 P	U	N	C	H

Clues Down.

1. Eaten with fish and chips.
2. Female sheep.
3. We eat their eggs for breakfast.
4. There are seven of these!
5. Never drop them!

GRAN and Mickey were playing 'snap'. Mickey had been losing the game for the past half hour and Gran had won a large pile of Atomic Thunderbusters. Gran put another card on the top of the others.

"Snap," she said, picking up another Atomic Thunderbuster.

"Oh fiddle," replied Mickey.

"I've never cheated in me life, Fluff," Gran commented.

Mickey decided he's had enough of this game. He never seemed to win. He asked Gran if they could go out and buy some new games to play. Gran thought it was a good idea. They would go immediately!

Once in the high street, Mickey became very excited. He liked shopping. They stopped outside the window of a very large store. The window was full of every toy imaginable. They walked inside and wandered to the games section. The display contained boxes of jigsaws, snakes and ladders, card games, dice games and dozens more. Gran finally settled for a box of dominoes. She took the box to the assistant who wrapped them in a brown paper bag and gave her a receipt for the money she had paid. Gran turned round to speak to Mickey but he had disappeared! She began to search for him.

Meanwhile, Mickey had wandered to the battery operated toys. He spoke to a very pretty doll, who immediately started to walk across the floor.

"My name is Angela," said the doll. "I love you mummy," she continued.

"Pretty neat," replied Mickey, "but I'm not your mummy, I'm Mickey!"

The doll walked straight past Mickey. Her arms were outstretched and as she walked she continued to chatter, "I love you mummy."

Mickey spoke to a large spotted dog. At the sound of Mickey's voice the dog wagged its tail and barked furiously. Very soon all the toys were walking, talking, barking and generally creating havoc in that section of the store.

Gran heard the commotion and found Mickey in the middle of it all!

"What are you doing, Fluff?" she asked Mickey.

"These are my new friends. This is my little Fruitbat," he said, addressing the toys.

A very angry shop assistant marched over to Gran, Mickey and the toys. Mickey stood still and the assistant thought he was one of the toys. She also thought Gran was responsible for the chaos. She sternly told Gran to leave the shop, turned her back and began to press all the 'off' buttons.

"Come on Fluff," said Gran, "I know when I'm not wanted!"

Mickey looked at the assistant, she was too busy to notice him. He followed Gran through the store and outside into the street. They hadn't gone very far when suddenly some-one put a hand on Gran's shoulder.

"You had better come with me," said the stranger.

"Not on your life!" exclaimed Gran, turning round to face a dark haired lady.

"I think you'd better do as I ask," continued the lady. "I'm the store detective, and I have reason to believe you have taken some goods from the toy shop without paying for them!"

Gran was cross at this suggestion and hit the lady with her umbrella.

"I've never taken anything without paying for it," she replied and opened her handbag to take out the bag of dominoes. "There," she said, "and here's my receipt!"

"Yes, yes," said the store detective impatiently, "we know about these little tricks. Pay for one small item and take a larger one. Though I must admit, you had a cheek thinking you could get away with this!"

"Get away with what?" Gran asked innocently.

"This," said the store detective, pointing to Mickey.

"You mean Fluff?" Gran asked laughing, "he came with me, we went to buy some dominoes!"

The store detective thought Gran was probably an eccentric or just plain 'nutty'. Now

she had heard everything! Taking a robot shopping indeed!

Gran prodded Mickey with her umbrella. "Tell her Fluff," she said. Mickey didn't move a nut or bolt. He stood completely still. This could be fun, he was thinking to himself.

A small van pulled up at the kerb side and a policeman jumped out. He had come to take Gran to the police station. The store detective and the policeman put Mickey into the back of the van. He was the evidence of Gran's 'crime'.

Gran was ushered into the front seat of the van. "Some-one will pay for this," she muttered.

"That's what it's all about," said the store detective. "I'll see you later, Bert," she said, addressing the policeman. The policeman nodded, started the van and took Gran and Mickey to the police station for questioning.

When they arrived at the police station, Gran and Mickey were taken to one of the cells. Mickey still remained silent in the corner of the cell where two policemen had, with great difficulty, placed him!

"I'm only a poor defenceless old woman," said Gran tearfully, dabbing her eyes with a handkerchief. "Take that," she said and hit the policeman with her umbrella.

"Hardly defenceless," muttered the policeman rubbing his shin bone where the umbrella had found its target!

The policeman pulled a note book and pencil from his pocket. He had to take a statement. The prospect didn't please him. What on earth did a little old Granny want with a robot anyway?

"Now," he began, "where do you live?"

"At home," replied Gran.

"Where is home?" asked the policeman.

"Home is where the heart is," said Gran and began to sing 'home, home on the range, where the deer and the antelope play!'

The policeman decided to try a different approach. "Do you live alone?"

" Course not," said Gran.

"Who lives with *you*?"

"Nobody!" Gran replied immediately.

The policeman groaned. "I thought you said you didn't live alone?" he said.

"I don't," said Gran impatiently.

"Then who do *you* live with?" asked the policeman getting more confused.

"My daughter, that's Margery, Her husband, he's my son-in-law you know. Then there's Haley, Steve and Ken, my grand-children and Mickey," Gran added.

"Who is Mickey?" asked the policeman, "the dog?"

Gran pointed to Mickey in the corner of the cell and told the policeman *he* was Mickey and that they had been shopping for dominoes because he didn't like playing 'snap' anymore!

"I'm back where I started," the policeman muttered to himself.

"I didn't think you'd been anywhere,"

commented Gran.

The policeman, feeling that he wasn't getting anywhere with this interview, decided to go and get Gran and himself a cup of tea.

Gran and Mickey were alone in the cell. Mickey had been listening to the conversation with great interest. He moved towards Gran.

"Hello, my little Fruitbat," he said quietly.

"What are you playing at?" asked Gran, "why didn't you tell that policeman I didn't steal you? I'm very cross," she concluded, although she didn't sound very cross.

"If they don't believe Super Gran, then why should they believe me?" Mickey asked wistfully.

Gran nodded. She had to agree. "We are in a heap of trouble, Fluff," she said. Mickey looked around the cell he couldn't see a heap of trouble anywhere!

"We'll have a game of dominoes," said Gran, "it will help to pass the time."

"Okey-doke," replied Mickey.

Gran took the dominoes out of the bag and laid them out on the table in the cell. They began to play. Mickey was very good. He thought it was a pity they didn't have any Thunderbusters to play for.

"Dominoes are pretty neat, huh?" Mickey asked Gran.

They heard the policeman returning to the cell and Mickey resumed his position in the corner. Two cups of tea were placed on the table and the policeman sat down. "Let's try again," he said to Gran.

"Do you fancy a game of dominoes?" Gran asked him. "I've just had a very good game with Mickey!"

The policeman looked at the dominoes, then at Gran, then at Mickey – silent and in the same place as when he left the cell.

"Robots don't play dominoes," said the policeman.

"Mickey isn't a robot, he's Mickey," replied Gran, "and he plays dominoes very well."

The policeman didn't see Mickey wink at Gran. He put his head in his hands and groaned very loudly, "shall we try to get this statement right?" he asked her again.

"Anything to oblige," said Gran smiling at the policeman and patting his hand. "Fire away!"

"What were you doing in the toy shop?"

"Shopping," Gran replied.

"Shop lifting, you mean?" the policeman suggested.

"Now do I look as though I could lift a shop, a poor defenceless old woman like me?" Gran said dabbing her eyes again.

The frustrated policeman decided he had better contact Gran's daughter.

"Is your daughter on the telephone?" he asked.

"Now how can I tell you that?" asked Gran. "I'm here and she's at home!"

"Does she have a telephone?" the

policeman shouted.

"Yes," shouted Gran, "and there's no need to shout, I'm not deaf!"

"That's all I wanted to know," he replied.

"Then why didn't you ask? Question – are you deaf? Answer – no!"

Feeling that if he stayed with Gran much longer, he would be as 'dotty' as she was, the policeman left the cell to phone the daughter. Perhaps, he should have done that earlier to save himself all this trouble.

"I'll phone your home and get your daughter to come down," he said.

Gran nodded. "I'll finish my game then," she replied and began to sort out the dominoes.

The policeman phoned Margery and told her about the case of Gran's shop lifting. On hearing the news Margery promptly fainted. Mr Wilberforce picked up the dangling telephone wondering what on earth had caused his wife to behave in such a manner! He was informed about Gran and told the policeman he would be at the station as soon as possible. The policeman hung up. At last he was getting somewhere! Or so he thought!

Mr. Wilberforce couldn't bring his wife out of her faint, so he put his jacket under her head to make her comfortable and then hurriedly left the house. He didn't have time to collect another jacket. He jumped into his car and roared off in the direction of the police station.

"As if I haven't enough troubles," he muttered to himself, as he drove off at an alarming speed.

A police patrol car passed him in the opposite direction.

"Well Bill, there's a regular lunatic if ever I saw one," the patrolman said to his partner. "C'mon, let's give chase."

The patrol car did an amazing 'U' turn and, siren blazing, gave chase on the unsuspecting Mr. Wilberforce.

Mr. Wilberforce heard the siren and saw the patrol car in his mirror.

"Didn't think I needed a police escort," he said to himself.

The patrol car pulled in front of Mr. Wilberforce and the large red 'STOP' sign lit up. Mr. Wilberforce braked suddenly. The car screamed to a halt. Bill, the patrolman stepped out of his car and walked over to Mr. Wilberforce.

"Well, if it isn't James Hunt," he said sarcastically.

"You're right, it isn't. Name's Wilberforce," said Mr. Wilberforce.

"I'll accompany you to the station," said Bill.

Mr. Wilberforce thanked him but said that he was perfectly capable of making his own way. The patrolman assured Mr. Wilberforce it was all in the interest of crime prevention and promptly opened the passenger door and climbed in. He waved the patrol car on and told Mr. Wilberforce to proceed to the station.

Mr. Wilberforce hastily sped through the traffic and in his hurry, drove straight through a traffic light that was on red. He hoped the patrolman hadn't noticed! It was only a minor slip up after all, and this was an emergency!

They stopped outside the police station and Bill, as quick as a flash appeared at the driver's door and helped Mr. Wilberforce out of the car.

"We'd better go straight to the charge office," said Bill.

Mr. Wilberforce nodded in agreement. The protective arm of the law was firmly gripping *his* arm. These officers certainly seemed to be doing their best for him!

Inside the office, the duty sergeant was busy with a mountain of paper work. He looked up when he heard the new arrivals.

"What's this then," said the sergeant, looking directly at Mr. Wilberforce.

"Your very kind officers have escorted me here to see my mother-in-law," said Mr. Wilberforce. "She's in your custody for shop lifting," he said lowering his voice to a mere whisper.

Bill, the patrolman looked at Mr. Wilberforce in amazement. "Mother-in-law here for shop lifting and you on three counts – he must think we are running a family guest house," he concluded looking at the two other policemen. The sergeant seemed confused. Mr. Wilberforce seemed confused, but then he really was confused. "Three counts?" he said.

"Exceeding the speed limit, driving without due care and attention, and failing to stop at a red light. How's that for a start?" said Bill.

Mr. Wilberforce groaned. "What about Gran?" he asked.

"She's downstairs in a cell with the metal robot she stole," replied the duty sergeant.

Mr. Wilberforce groaned once more. "Oh no, not again," he said.

"You mean she's done something like this before?" asked the sergeant.

"No of course not," Mr. Wilberforce said, "It's that robot. He's the one to blame!"

"I see sir," said the sergeant adopting a more patronizing tone.

The sergeant was beginning to think the whole family were 'dotty' if Gran and Mr. Wilberforce were anything to go by! He told Bert, the policeman who had been interviewing Gran, to take Mr. Wilberforce down to her cell. They would settle the driving offences later!

Gran and Mickey had played several good games of dominoes. Gran had even persuaded a young police officer to bring her some fish and chips and a pot of tea. She was rather enjoying the hospitality of the force! Mickey too was enjoying the fact that he kept winning the games.

"Not had so much fun in ages," said Gran.

"And more to come, my little Fruitbat," said Mickey, "because Bootface has just arrived. He'll be down in a minute!"

"Wish I had your sensitive ears, Fluff. You don't miss a thing!"

Mr. Wilberforce and the policeman entered the cell. Mickey adopted his silent pose once more.

Mr. Wilberforce marched into the cell and faced Mickey. "This is your fault, you . . . you, monstrous, metallic, maniac, you mendacious, mercurial, machine, you . . . you . . ." The words hung in mid-sentence. Mr.

Wilberforce had run out of insults!

"Verbal indigestion can catch you out," said Mickey and swivelled his head round.

The policeman looked at Mickey in amazement. "It spoke," he said.

"Pretty neat, huh?" Mickey said. "Pleased to meet you P.C. Bert. I'm Mickey." Mickey held out an arm. Bert shook hands. He seemed to be in a daze. Suddenly, he realised what he was doing. "Shaking hands with a robot," he muttered, "whatever next!"

"Anyway what are you doing here?" said Gran to Mr. Wilberforce.

"What do you think I'm doing here," said Mr. Wilberforce, "I'm Elvis Presley dressed in a gold lamè suit and singing 'Jailhouse Rock' ".

Mickey decided it was time for some real fun! With a little Metal Mickey magic ... things began to happen! Mr. Wilberforce ran his fingers through his hair, took up an Elvis pose and began to gyrate his hips in time to his strained attempts at singing ... "Went to a party at the county jail," he began.

"Boogie-boogie," said Metal Mickey and started to boogie around the cell. Gran clapped her hands. "C'mon Fluff, hit it!"

Bert, the policeman looked on in amazement. Nothing quite like this had ever happened to him before. "What's going on?" he shrieked.

"He's Elvis the Pelvis!" exclaimed Gran, tears of laughter streaming down her face.

"If he's Elvis then I'm the Incredible Hulk," he replied, turning slightly green. With a sudden burst of amazing strength, he smashed the table with one blow of his fist! Mickey's magic powers were at work once more!

The prison cell was a riot! Gran was fighting off the Incredible Hulk, using her umbrella as a weapon. Mr. Wilberforce was still dancing and singing. Mickey was boogieing around the wreckage!

The duty sergeant came rushing downstairs to the cell. "I'm going 'bananas'," he shouted, surveying the chaos around him!

"Sure are," said Mickey mischievously. His

magical powers were in full swing.

The duty sergeant was last seen dashing from the cell, in the shape of a huge banana wearing size twelve boots and a policeman's helmet!

W.P.C. Madge Bentley arrived at the police station to commence her shift. There was no-one in the office. She heard the commotion downstairs and went to investigate. As she entered the wrecked cell, Mickey released Bert and Mr. Wilberforce from his power. The two of them looked at the baffled Madge. "Where is the duty sergeant?" she asked. No-one appeared to know. They all looked at Mickey. "Remember that large banana, Mush?" he said to Bert. Bert nodded slowly, it was all coming back to him now. He groaned, "Oh, no, don't tell me . . .?"

Madge decided to take control of the situation. "You can all go home," she said, "including you, Bert." Bert nodded numbly. He needed a rest. He must be working under too much strain. Perhaps a month in the Bahamas . . .?

Mr. Wilberforce addressed the policewoman. "I appear to, er, have, er, some driving, er, offences," he stuttered.

"We'll sort that out later," she replied, in a hurry to get rid of them all before something mysterious happened again!

Gran picked up the dominoes, her handbag and umbrella. "C'mon Fluff, it's time for off!"

"Okey-doke," replied Mickey. "Goodbye cheeky chops," he said to Bert.

"Goodbye lovely police lady. Goodbye Bootface!"

Mr. Wilberforce couldn't leave the cell quick enough. "I'm coming with you," he said to Gran and Mickey.

"No fear," said Gran, "you're a criminal. All those driving offences! Mickey and me will make our own way home! Come on Fluff, we don't want to be among jailbirds! After all we are innocent!"

Mickey trundled after Gran. They were going home. They would be able to play some more games of dominoes and this time using Atomic Thunderbusters for stakes! He could hardly wait!

FLOWER POWER

MR. W. HAS A BRILLIANT IDEA........?
OF COURSE, THAT'S IT, STEVE'S BIKE – I CAN CYCLE TO WORK IN A JIFFY!
SO.......
AAARGGH!
NOT RIDDEN A BIKE IN TWENTY YEARS – BUT THEY TELL ME YOU NEVER FORGET. IT'S AS EASY AS FALLING OFF A LOG!
AND IT IS! ......
EVENTUALLY.........
NOT BAD FOR AN OLD......... ER..... MIDDLE-AGED CHAP LIKE ME!
.... HE'S ON HIS WAY TO WORK!
DAD WILL BE PLEASED YOU CAN DO THE JOB.
ME TOO, I COULD DO WITH THE WORK, AND THE MONEY!
MRW 31 W
GOODBYE CECIL, MY POOR LITTLE DAMAGED FRIEND
LATER THAT EVENING......
.... SO, I'VE HAD THE CAR TOWED TO THE GARAGE, IT BELONGS TO A PAL OF MINE – SHOULDN'T COST MUCH TO REPAIR – ABOUT FIVE HUNDRED POUNDS. BUT THEN THERE'S THE LAMP-POST AND BUS STOP
WHICH REMINDS ME DEAR...... YOU HAVEN'T PAID THEM. THIS CAME TODAY!
GROAN, THOUGHT THEY'D BE COVERED BY THE 'RATES'.
PRETTY NEAT, HUH!

SOME DAYS LATER STEVE DECIDES TO SEE HOW DAD'S CAR REPAIRS ARE PROGRESSING
I WANT TO GO, MUST SEE MY FRIEND CECIL
CECIL? WHO'S HE?
BOOTFACE'S CAR, WHO ELSE?
HELLO CECIL, I'M HERE AS PROMISED. YOU LOOK PRETTY NEAT HUH?
DON'T LIKE THE NEW COAT – I LOOK LIKE EVERYONE ELSE AROUND HERE! ALL THESE DRAB COLOURS!
MICKEY TAKES A LOOK AT THE OTHER CARS – CECIL IS RIGHT – THEY'RE ALL THE SAME!
WHILE STEVE CHATS TO HIS MECHANIC FRIEND, MICKEY HAS AN IDEA.........
FLOWERS ARE NICE, THE BOOTFACE LIKES FLOWERS, GRAN LIKES FLOWERS, LITTLE DIPPY LIKES FLOWERS. DO YOU LIKE FLOWERS CECIL?
FLOWERS ARE COLOURFUL, NOT DRAB LIKE ME.
IN A CORNER OF THE GARAGE, MICKEY SPOTS A COMPRESSOR AND SEVERAL CANS OF PAINT..............
... WITH A LITTLE METAL MICKEY MAGIC.....
BUTTERCUPS AND DAISIES, BLUEBELLS AND ROSES.......
I FEEL BETTER ALREADY
CECIL, BOOTFACE'S CAR, IS GETTING A VERY SPECIAL METAL MICKEY TYPE RE-SPRAY.
...... AND GREEN LEAVES, AND BUTTERFLIES AND BUMBLE-BEES
WOW! THIS IS GREAT, I'LL BE THE TALK OF THE TOWN
YOU BET, BOOGIE-BOOGIE! BOOTFACE IS IN FOR A SURPRISE
.... AND STEVE....?
CAN I LOOK AT THE CAR NOW
SURE, IT'S OVER HERE, I'VE DONE A GOOD JOB, THOUGH I SAY IT MYSELF. YOU'LL BE SURPRISED
HE SURE WILL!!!!!....

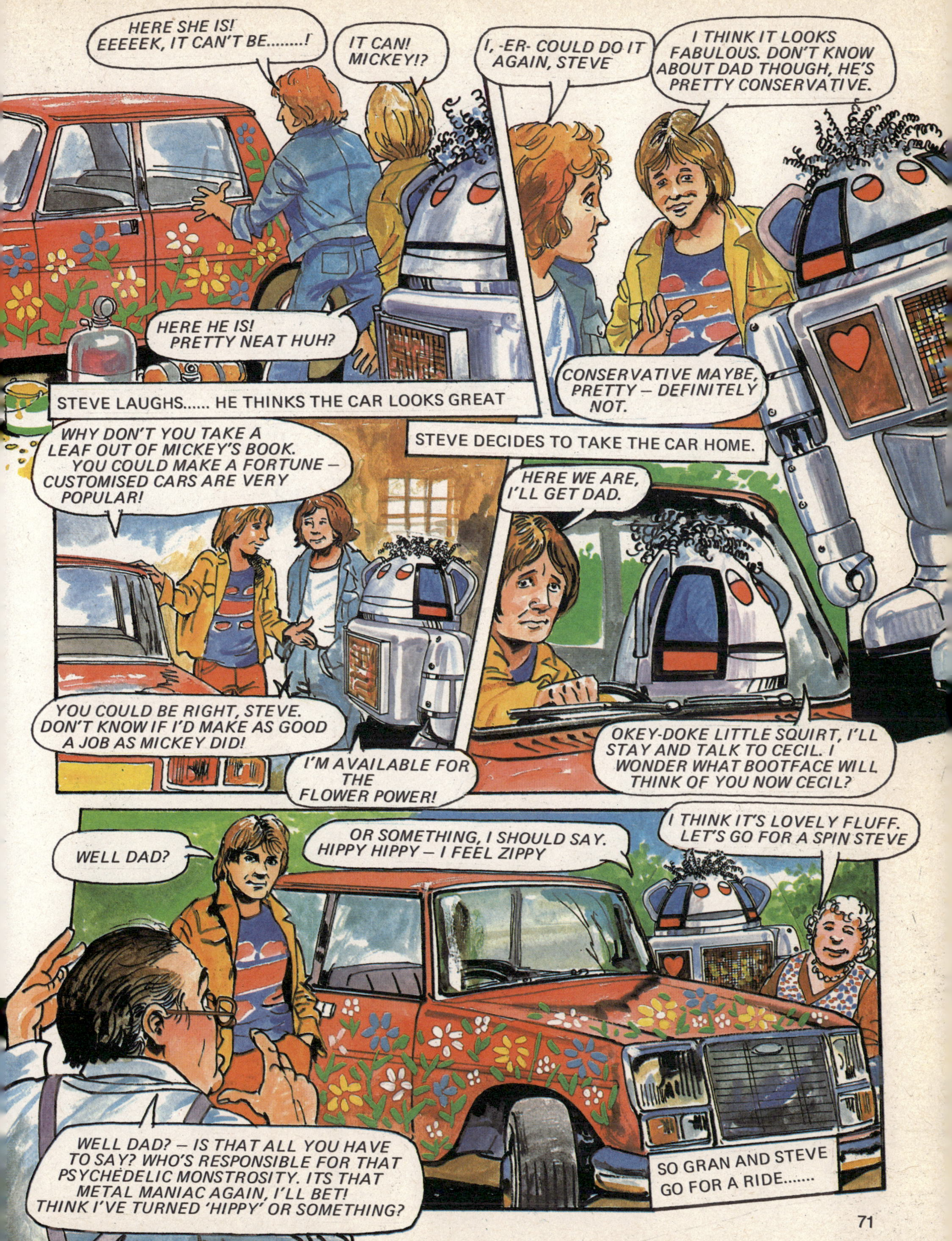
HERE SHE IS! EEEEEK, IT CAN'T BE........!
IT CAN! MICKEY!?
HERE HE IS! PRETTY NEAT HUH?
STEVE LAUGHS...... HE THINKS THE CAR LOOKS GREAT
I, -ER- COULD DO IT AGAIN, STEVE
I THINK IT LOOKS FABULOUS. DON'T KNOW ABOUT DAD THOUGH, HE'S PRETTY CONSERVATIVE.
CONSERVATIVE MAYBE, PRETTY – DEFINITELY NOT.
WHY DON'T YOU TAKE A LEAF OUT OF MICKEY'S BOOK. YOU COULD MAKE A FORTUNE – CUSTOMISED CARS ARE VERY POPULAR!
YOU COULD BE RIGHT, STEVE. DON'T KNOW IF I'D MAKE AS GOOD A JOB AS MICKEY DID!
I'M AVAILABLE FOR THE FLOWER POWER!
STEVE DECIDES TO TAKE THE CAR HOME.
HERE WE ARE, I'LL GET DAD.
OKEY-DOKE LITTLE SQUIRT, I'LL STAY AND TALK TO CECIL. I WONDER WHAT BOOTFACE WILL THINK OF YOU NOW CECIL?
WELL DAD?
WELL DAD? – IS THAT ALL YOU HAVE TO SAY? WHO'S RESPONSIBLE FOR THAT PSYCHEDELIC MONSTROSITY. ITS THAT METAL MANIAC AGAIN, I'LL BET! THINK I'VE TURNED 'HIPPY' OR SOMETHING?
OR SOMETHING, I SHOULD SAY. HIPPY HIPPY – I FEEL ZIPPY
I THINK IT'S LOVELY FLUFF. LET'S GO FOR A SPIN STEVE
SO GRAN AND STEVE GO FOR A RIDE.......

PASSERSBY WAVE TO GRAN AND STEVE
I FEEL LIKE THE QUEEN MUM. EVERYONE'S LOOKING AT US!
IT'S THE CAR THAT'S CAUSING THE SENSATION GRAN.
THE LIGHTS CHANGE, AS THE CAR STOPS A MAN APPROACHES.....
GEE WHAT A FANTASTIC CAR! WHAT DO YOU WANT FOR IT?
WE'RE IN THE MONEY STEVE!
CAR SOLD, MONEY SPENT!
PHEW! DIDN'T THINK ME LEGS WOULD CARRY ME HOME.
ME NEITHER. WHAT A LOT OF PRESENTS.
PRESENTS! BOOGIE-BOOGIE.
KNOCK AT THE DOOR
YOUR NEW CAR'S ARRIVED DAD.
WHAT NEW CAR? I CAN'T AFFORD A NEW CAR!
YOU DID?
WE'VE SOLD FLOWER POWER CECIL AND MADE A HUGE PROFIT!

EVERYONE GOES TO LOOK AT THE NEW CAR ......
WOW BOOGIE-BOOGIE, HELLO LOVELY LADY — I'M MICKEY
WOW! ANOTHER CHANCE TO BE A BUDDING ARTIST.......!
ZIPPP!
BANG!
.... A LITTLE METAL MICKEY MAGIC.
JUMPING JACKS AND CATHERINE WHEELS, FLUFF......
BANG
POW!
TELL ME WHY DO YOU DO THESE THINGS? DO YOU THINK I'M GUY FAWKES?
BANG
THE IDEA'S APPEALING, BOOGIE-BOOGIE.........
GUNPOWDER, TREASON AND PLOT! TO THE HOUSES OF PARLIAMENT............
BOOGIE-BOOGIE, PRETTY NEAT, HUH?

The Amazomatic Pud!

Metal Mickey has devised the most amazomatic Pud you can imagine. He is singing his version of the Twelve Days of Christmas which is printed on the following page. His super powers and Metal Mickey magic are the main ingredients for his Pud which he says will make the day go like a bomb!

Ingredients for Amazomatic Pud –

7 kilos flour
24 eggs (poached, scrambled fried or boiled)
1 basket (to keep all your eggs in)
2 birds in a bush (or one in the hand will do)
12 oranges
6 lemons
sack lime
sack cement
sack saltpeter
sack charcoal
pinch salt (make sure it doesn't pinch you back)
Brandy (from Bootface's cocktail cabinet)
5 kilos yeast
1 kilo coarse metal filings
5 metres 52 ohm coax
10 packets Atomic Thunderbusters
As many sub-standard magnetic antenna's as available
6 bottles coca cola
7 lords a leaping
6 maids a milking
2 choir boys
sprig of holly or plastic father christmas (from last years christmas pudding)

Method.

Take a very large bowl or alternatively remove all the coal from the bath. If the latter, rinse well. Put flour, eggs (all in one basket), birds (if using only one remove the hand first), oranges, lemons, lime, cement, saltpeter, yeast, salt.

Get 7 lords to leap up and down in mixture until blended together.

Drink two bottles of coca cola.

Cut 1 metre coax and fillet it. (save until later)

Drink two more bottles of coca cola. (you have only two left)

Add coarse metal filings and blend in milk (obtained from 6 maids a milking)

Send 7 lords a leaping back to their own song.

Reinforce the mess – mixture! – with as many sub-standard magnetic antenna's and ten atomic thunderbusters.

Gift wrap and tie with remaining coax. Inscribe with legendary message 'Merry Xmas'.

Put filleted coax in a fuse like manner into top of Pud. Cook for 3 hours or until set. During this time drink two bottles of coca cola (there are now none left) and sing many versions, ie verses, of the Twelve Days of Christmas with the two choir boys. (songs printed overleaf) You can boogie as well but remember the six bottles of very fizzy coca cola...! When the Pud is done to a turn, turn around and pour a large glass of brandy down the filleted coax on top of Pud. The amazomatic pud is now complete. After the main course on Christmas day, the Pud is ready to serve.

Coca-Cola
TRADE MARK R
CHAR
Serving Instructions (to be followed with great care)
Place one of the Christmas candles as close as possible to the filleted coax containing brandy and STAND WELL BACK.
The Pud will blow up and everyone will get a lump..... on the head, arms, legs etc. Of course the Pud doesn't really exist, it's just A FILIMENT IN METAL MICKEY'S IMAGINATION!

The Twelve Days of Christmas etc...

To be sung to the tune of Twelve Days of Christmas – if you don't know it improvise!

On the twelfth day of Christmas Mickey sent to me .....

12 tweeters tweeting
11 flashbulbs flashing
10 Atomic Thunderbusters
9 duff transistors
8 carbide batteries
7 sticks of solder
6 silicon chips
5 nuts and bolts (remember tune changes here!)
4 coax leads
3 cans of oil
2 boogie-boogies
and a partridge in a pear tree (the originality of the song is maintained here!)

The above is only the chorus, to get the best enjoyment from the song start at the end and finish at the beginning. It sounds better that way too!

ANSWERS

WHAT'S IN A NAME?

Tale	Cake	Like	Kate	Tack
Mail	Take	Lack	Item	Meet
Team	Make	Mice	Mate	Lime
Late	Meal	Lice	Mite	Mime
Lame	Meat	Tame	Time	Meek
Lake	Mike	Kite	Tail	Clay

CROSSWORD

1 P	2 U	3 N	4 C	5 H
6 P	U	N	C	H
7 P	U	N	C	H
8 P	U	N	C	H
9 P	U	N	C	H

HAVE A METAL MICKEY CHRISTMAS AND A ZIPPY, PRETTY NEAT NEW YEAR!

mickey's metropolis

1

2

3

4

5